BUNGALOW BASICS
FIREPLACES

By Paul Duchscherer

Photography by Douglas Keister

Pomegranate

SAN FRANCISCO

Published by Pomegranate Communications, Inc.
Box 6099, Rohnert Park, California 94927
800-227-1428; www.pomegranate.com

Pomegranate Europe Ltd.
Unit 1, Heathcote Business Centre, Hurlbutt Road
Warwick, Warwickshire CV34 6TD, U. K.

Library of Congress Cataloging-in-Publication Data
Duchscherer, Paul.
    Bungalow basics. Fireplaces / text by Paul Duchscherer ; photographs by
Douglas Keister.
        p. cm.
    ISBN 0-7649-2213-0 (alk. paper)
    1. Fireplaces. 2. Bungalows. I. Title: Fireplaces. II. Keister, Douglas. III. Title.

    TH7424 .D83 2003
    749'.62–dc21

                                                                2002030741

Pomegranate Catalog No. A658

Designed by Patrice Morris

Printed in Korea

12 11 10 09 08 07 06 05 04 03   10 9 8 7 6 5 4 3 2 1

This book is dedicated to the discovery,
appreciation, and preservation of bungalows,
and especially to all those who
love and care for them.

Acknowledgments

Because of space limitations, we regret that it is not possible to acknowledge each of those individuals and organizations who have helped us with this book. Our heartfelt appreciation is extended especially to all the homeowners who, by graciously sharing their homes with us, have made this book a reality. Special thanks are given also to Sandy Schweitzer, John Freed, and Don Merrill for their tireless support, unflagging encouragement, and invaluable assistance. We salute you!

Space constraints also preclude us from listing every credit due to each deserving and talented artisan, architect, designer, craftsperson, and manufacturer whose work appears in this book. We offer them our deepest gratitude for the opportunity to include it here. Alternatively, our readers may wish to consult the extensive credit listings in our earlier book series, published by Penguin Putnam Inc. (comprising *The Bungalow: America's Arts & Crafts Home, Inside the Bungalow: America's Arts & Crafts Interior,* and *Outside the Bungalow: America's Arts & Crafts Garden*), which make reference to many of the images that are also included in this book.

BUNGALOW BASICS

Ever since an American icon of idealized domesticity (the bungalow) hooked up with the ultimate symbol of hearth and home (the fireplace), a mutual love affair has kept them nearly inseparable. The compact scale of the bungalow only exaggerates the importance and visibility of its fireplace.

It is difficult to imagine bungalows without fireplaces, but they do exist. They tend to be the smallest ones, especially the dollhouse-sized dwellings in little compounds called bungalow courts, which were first developed as seasonal rentals (or affordable starter homes) in warm climates. With barely a square foot to spare, these miniatures are nonetheless enormously appealing even today for their ability to evoke (as bigger bungalows do) a priceless sense of "home."

While some standard-sized bungalows were built without fireplaces, probably only the builder benefited from omitting them. Most occupants of such houses feel that something is missing. Whether or not Americans grew up with fireplaces in their homes, the allure of having one was surely amplified by experiences in places such as summer cabins and ski lodges, where a cozy fire seemed indispensable. It is not surprising that fireplaces, which could evoke such positive emotions, loomed large in the marketing agenda of bungalow plan book purveyors, builders, and real estate developers.

Was there some truth to their ecstatic claims of the bungalow's legion virtues? Certainly. Although claims of enhanced familial bliss were outlandish, most people who bought into the "bungalow dream" were not disappointed. After all, qualities of affordability, good planning, and convenience were combined with the newest kitchen and bath technologies of the era. At the end of their working day, many families could indeed stare into their glowing fireplaces and happily count their blessings.

Considering the staggering number of bungalows that were built across the country, there are now several generations of people who grew up in them. Countless other people spent lots of time visiting the homes of friends or relatives fortunate enough to occupy bungalows. Hardships of the Great Depression notwithstanding, Americans share many collective memories of bungalows, and most tend to be good ones. Such reassuring memories often include the comforting vision of a bungalow fireplace.

Today's revival of interest in bungalows has included a renewed look at their fireplaces. A flurry of activity in restoration and renovation of these houses has created a demand for putting back what might be missing, or, in some cases, putting in something better (see Figure 1). While decisions to change original features may have negative consequences, replacing a missing or misaligned fireplace has positive ones. Before making final design decisions, an owner needs to "listen" carefully to the existing architecture of the house, for any new fireplace design will be affected by the materials, detailing, and proportions of the room around it.

One favorite bungalow fireplace configuration, known as an inglenook (*ingle* derives from a Gaelic word for fire), is perhaps the ultimate in coziness (Figures 6 to 11). By general definition, inglenooks are fireplace alcoves or recesses with flanking built-in benches. Although an inglenook uses more space than a fireplace alone, some of the smallest bungalows were originally designed with them. Adding an inglenook to an existing structure is difficult, but any-one building a new home should consider the possibility of working one into the plans. They vary widely in size and quality of finish, and an inglenook need not be large to have considerable impact.

Most bungalows had a single fireplace, which tended to be the focal point of the living room. Usually it had a thick wood mantel above a fac-ing, or surround, of masonry (brick or stone) or ceramic tile (Figure 2). Craftsman-style fireplaces commonly were combined with built-ins; many had pairs of glass-fronted bookcases or benches (or a combina-tion of the two) to either side (Figures 14, 22, 35, and 36). Beyond these basic configurations, fireplace mantels and their related surface materials were combined and presented in a remarkable array of forms.

The most common fireplace material was brick, and many bunga-low fireplaces used the simplest varieties. Colors typically ranged from reds to brownish tans to yellowish buffs. Although some people find plain brick colors uninteresting, they can be a striking part of a well-designed, nicely proportioned fireplace (Figures 5, 6, 9, 24, and 26). Sometimes solid-colored brick was combined with ceramic tile accents (Figures 39 and 41) or set with bricks of contrasting color and texture into a pattern, for added interest (Figures 31 and 32). Especially popular during the Craftsman era and found in many bungalows (inside and out), clinker brick has rich colors and textures (Figures 21, 25, and 27). Prior to 1900, most clinker bricks were considered discards or seconds at brick factories, because they result from overheating in the kiln (the name supposedly derives from clinking sounds made during the process), which causes the surface of common red brick to begin to vitrify (melt), warp, and deepen in color. Architects with an Arts and Crafts sensibility found clinker brick appealing and used it to produce rustic, organic effects on fireplaces and chimneys. A classic Craftsman bungalow treatment for exterior applications (such as foundations and porch columns) employed clinker brick with river rock in striking combinations. Nicknamed peanut-brittle-style masonry, it was seen especially around Pasadena, California, and favored by architects Greene and Greene.

Another favorite bungalow fireplace material was natural stone. Perhaps no other material can evoke the feeling of rusticity so successfully. While various types were used (with regional differences due to availability), one of the most popular was smooth-textured, rounded river rock, sometimes called cobble (Figures 15 and 19). Massive, rough-edged slabs of fieldstone were also used, to create fireplaces and chimneys that sometimes towered to the ceiling (Figures 12 to 14). Not all stone was exactly as it appeared. Advanced concrete technology of the period produced "cast stone" materials that not only could mimic the look of rough stone slabs and fieldstone blocks but also could be used for refined accents, including low-relief pictorial panels (Figures 16 to 18).

Closely vying with brick and stone effects in popularity was the use of handmade ceramic tile for bungalow fireplaces. Often large tiles were used to face the fireplace below a wooden mantel (Figures 35 and 38). Tile offered an even greater range of colors and textures than stone or brick. Craftsman designers were partial to matte-finished glazes in an Arts and Crafts palette of muted, earthy colors. Many glaze treatments mixed more than one color, with the results sometimes resembling art-pottery glazes of the period. Textural effects created by dripping glazes were highly prized for their "natural" beauty (Figures 46 and 47). Among the most favored Craftsman tile palettes were shades of dark green, as in Figures 48 and 49. Widely imitated by other manufacturers of the era, famed tile maker Ernest Batchelder produced a popular line of matte-finished tiles in soft colors in the 1920s. To complement their shaded, antiqued appearance, Batchelder (and others) offered coordinated moldings and accent pieces such as pictorial tiles, corbels, and keystones, as shown in Figures 37 and 41 to 43. A growing restoration market for bungalow fireplaces has influenced today's ceramic tile industry, which once again is producing appropriate designs for period houses (Figures 1, 4, and 40). A vibrant part of the Arts and Crafts revival, leading ceramic suppliers for restorations tend to be small companies (or individual artisans) specializing in handmade or hand-finished tiles. Many of their creations are equal in quality to the best of the originals.

A number of period bungalow fireplaces have been neglected over the years and require expert attention to ensure that they are working safely and properly; some may need to be entirely reconstructed. A fairly common problem is smoke overflow from the fireplace opening. This often can be helped or entirely corrected by adding a small projecting hood. If a hood is aesthetically appropriate for the fireplace, it can present an opportunity to introduce hand-hammered copper or handwrought iron or steel as part of its design (Figures 4, 21, and 27 to 30). Some fireplaces have been successfully retrofitted with gas-powered concrete logs, which eliminate smoke and cleaning problems. Many otherwise intact period fireplaces are remodeled with more heat-efficient inserts, but their overall design is likely to suffer. Short of removing the insert and starting over, one possible remedy is to find an especially beautiful (preferably handmade) metal fire screen and simply hide the unappealing insert when the fireplace is not in use, as in Figure 17.

BUNGALOW BASICS

The bungalow fireplaces that fill this book are successful working examples showing how a variety of styles, materials, and techniques combine to create some of the period's most alluring interior features. For people considering new work, especially in the Craftsman style, nothing inspires so well as these original models. Fireplaces with period designs that have been enhanced by repair or replacement of some finish materials can teach another lesson. In concert with its house, each fireplace should make a style statement that is an individual, perhaps unique, expression of its gentle presence. An essential symbol of hearth and home (more a state of mind than anything tangible), the fireplace is an intrinsic part of the celebrated legacy of Arts and Crafts design that is splendidly expressed in so many bungalows. Because they invite us to pause and reflect, these fireplaces remind us that American bungalows are treasures, and each one deserves to be cherished and preserved for future generations to discover and enjoy. ❦

❦ 1. Revealed as the front door swings open is a Craftsman-style mantel of quartersawn oak, featuring a beveled mirror, two display shelves set between squared columns, and a new handmade ceramic tile surround. In a major remodel of a long-neglected bungalow, the mantel and front door installed here were retrieved from a salvage yard and carefully restored. Now they augment the owner's collection of fine Arts and Crafts period furnishings.

Rug by Blue Hills Studio; tile by Tile Restoration Center

❦ 2 & 3. Illustrations in a 1912 design advice book, *Home Building and Decoration,* these two crisply rendered Craftsman-style room settings reveal typical bungalow features. The living room's beamed ceiling and built-ins (top illustration) complement the simple fireplace design, consisting of a bracketed wood mantel and paneled sides, surrounding a pale brick facing and hearth of glazed ceramic tile. On the library's fireplace (bottom illustration), a rustic facing and hearth using natural stones of varying sizes contrasts with a more refined built-in arrangement over the mantel. Flanking two glass-fronted bookcases, a pair of display cabinets with doors of leaded and beveled glass in a geometric pattern create a framed recess for the painting between them. Both rooms show the harmonious effect of a muted, medium-value wall color that does not contrast too strongly with the dark stain of the woodwork.

Archival images from the collection of Timothy Hansen and Dianne Ayres, Arts & Crafts Period Textiles

❦ 4. Although entirely open to the rest of the room, this arrangement of a central fireplace flanked by built-in seating creates the effect of an inglenook. Unifying the space is a high wood wainscot with an oversized dentil molding below its plate rail. Unlike hollow box beams, which are more commonly used, the solid Douglas fir beams in this 1910 Craftsman home are structural. Recent additions to the living room include the handmade tile surround and hearth, a hammered copper hood, and linen window shades and matching pillows stenciled by the owners.

🐾 5. Configured much like half an inglenook, this massive brick fireplace with its adjacent built-in seating, set opposite the front door, makes an inviting first impression. The stepped corbels supporting both mantel and box beams, a typical Craftsman-style detail, demonstrate the versatility of simple brick. Above the built-in benches are leaded glass windows, which open to allow more air circulation into a hallway to the bedrooms.

❧ 6. Placed to be seen upon entry, this 1906 inglenook is enclosed in one corner of a living room. Originally designed to burn coal for heat, the diminutive arched fireplace shows contrasting textures of limestone-colored brick. Colonial Revival influence is apparent in the classical molding details below the mantel, in the use of columns, and in the curving bench arms. Matched to traces of original color found behind some moldings, the warm eucalyptus green wall paint blends well with the amber gumwood trim and light maple floors.

🐾 7. From its recessed alcove, this inglenook can be seen from the rooms on either side of the pocket door at right. In addition to a full-width mantel and small display shelves, the fireplace has its original large square tile facing; the earthy palette and mottled matte finish were popular in the Craftsman era. The seats of the built-in benches lift up for access to storage, a typical feature.

8. In the living room of Pasadena's celebrated Gamble House, a 1908 master-work by famed architects Greene and Greene, this inglenook is a key part of one of the finest surviving examples of American Arts and Crafts design. Generously wide high-backed benches and display cabinets flank the broad, artistically tiled facing of the fireplace. Now open to the public as a house museum, the Gamble House retains its original furnishings and fittings throughout.

🐾 9. With its elevated floor, this classic Craftsman-style inglenook commands a position at one end of the living room like a small stage. Nicely backlit by the large casement windows framing the fireplace, a pair of sizable squared columns and spindled railings give the two built-in benches behind them a cozy sense of enclosure. The severity of the plain brick fireplace is relieved by a shallow recess above it, which is anchored by a thick wooden mantel set on oversized corbels.

🐨 10. Situated off one end of a living room, this unusually large 1912 inglenook creates a room within a room. The simplicity of the brick fireplace, with its chunky wood mantel and brackets, contrasts with the dramatic sweep of the arched opening. Centered on a wooden keystone, the arch spans two pairs of squared columns and built-in cabinets with leaded glass doors. Within the inglenook are more built-in shelves, seating, and a door leading to a back hall.

🐾 11. Placed lengthwise in a living room, this inglenook has a shallow depth that is offset by its generous width. Only partly screened to either side by pairs of massive square columns and low, paneled walls that conceal two built-in benches, the fireplace can be viewed from most of the room. To offset the strong, straight lines of the room's Craftsman-style detailing, the river rock of the fireplace contributes random rounded forms with natural color and texture.

❧ 12. *(left)* Original to a 1910 log house, this fieldstone-faced fireplace has a rustic, homey quality that recalls the ambience of a mountain lodge or perhaps the American colonial period. The wide, arched opening conjures up thoughts of cooking over the flames, while the oversized hearth would allow several people to huddle near the fire's warmth. A split-log mantel, set on log-end corbels, underlines the tapering stone chimney breast.

❧ 13. *(above)* Featured in a 1915 design advice book, this living room centers on a fireplace with a sloping chimney built of irregularly shaped stones. The board-and-batten backs of the built-in benches match the adjacent wainscoting. While the room is mostly in Craftsman style, the form and finish of the fireplace, the diamond-paned casement windows, and some of the room's accessories evoke a Colonial Revival quaintness. Curiously, several of the textile patterns seen here anticipate futuristic Art Deco style.

Archival image from the collection of Timothy Hansen and Dianne Ayres,
Arts & Crafts Period Textiles

🦌 14. *(left)* The slate-gray stone of this fireplace may have been quarried on-site during construction of the house in 1910. Arranged more massively below the mantel, the stone tapers above to align with a pair of box beams at the ceiling. The adjacent built-in cabinets, multipaned windows, and beam-mounted pendant lights are all original.

🦌 15. *(above)* Taken from a 1921 catalog published by the Morgan Company, this photograph shows a fireplace design and adjacent built-in bookcases that were available by mail order to both builders and home-owners. Modest homes commonly were fitted not with costly custom-built cabinets but rather with built-ins (as well as doors, hardware, and lighting) chosen from such catalogs. Only the wooden elements were shipped; the river rock facing was to be procured locally and assembled on-site.

Archival image from the collection of Timothy Hansen and Dianne Ayres, Arts & Crafts Period Textiles

🐚 16. Although this early-twentieth-century living room features walls and ceiling made entirely of Douglas fir, its ruggedly imposing stone fireplace has no wooden elements. On closer inspection, the design resembles some very convincing examples made of cast stone (a refined version of concrete) that were popular for the bungalow market. Sold in kits, carefully numbered pieces of "stone" would be assembled on-site according to a detailed diagram.

🐝 17. Fabricated entirely of cast stone, this rough-hewn fireplace features a pair of curiously shaped corbels resembling huge stylized acorns (or inverted bells), which support a thick mantel. Such picturesque design effects, responding to the public's taste for novelty, were fairly cheap to manufacture and easy to sell by catalog, so they appeared in modest bungalows across the country.

❦ 18. The full potential of cast stone artistry for fireplaces is apparent in this unusual period example, which incorporates a very refined low-relief pictorial panel across its face. Set in a framework of weighty, rough-cast horizontal and vertical elements, the sculptured panel depicts a landscape with a dreamy view of the eighteenth-century Santa Barbara Mission and evokes an early California mood.

🎗 19. Towering over one end of this Craftsman-style living room, a river rock fireplace shows the handiwork of a skilled mason. Large contrasting stones are placed around the fireplace opening, while the remaining stones appear to be positioned according to size: larger ones set below the mantel graduate to the smallest ones placed above it. Built-in seating in the far corner creates a partial inglenook.

❧ 20. In a contemporary interpretation of Craftsman style, a freestanding river rock fireplace has been positioned to face the living room while forming a rather sculptural screen for the dining room behind it. With its dual-level mantel, the tapering form of the fireplace allows openness and light between the adjoining areas, illustrating the versatility of Craftsman style in new construction.

🐨 21. Unless it is made of clinker brick (like this 1905 example), an all-brick fireplace can seem a bit too plain. The result of an overheated brick oven, clinker bricks were once sold as seconds (or discarded), until their unusual rich colors and craggy textures were discovered by architects and favored for their Craftsman-style projects. The bronze smoke guard with pierced squares has been added.

22. With its built-ins, box beam ceiling, leaded art-glass windows, and two-toned-brick fireplace, this 1909 living room is a Craftsman bungalow classic. The handsome, arched fireplace design shows how a few well-chosen variations in the color and texture of plain brick can make a big difference in impact. Recently, this brickwork and all the room's woodwork were laboriously stripped of many layers of white paint.

🐨 23. With its brick chimney stepped like a ziggurat, this fireplace, circa 1910, seems less massive than it really is. Its central placement allows a stairway to rise behind it at right. The raised hearth, not typical for the period, has an iron strap binding its upper edges. Continuing the line of the mantel to the left, an attached spindled screen with an art-glass panel separates the dining room yet keeps it open.

🐨 24. Both the diamond-paned windows set to either side of this fireplace and the steeply angled pitch of the brickwork above the mantel draw their inspiration from various European and American colonial sources. Here such historicism is added to the more straightforward Craftsman style to satisfy popular taste for a reassuringly familiar "quaintness."

🐝 25. *(overleaf, left)* In a spectacular ascent, the clinker brick chimney of the 1904 C. Hart Merriam House in the San Francisco Bay Area rises through a second floor mezzanine overlooking the living room. An arched fireplace opening relieves the preponderance of straight lines in the voluminous, all-redwood interior space. Built as a summer home for the renowned anthropologist and naturalist, this house shows elegant Craftsman-style restraint.

🐝 26. *(overleaf, right)* Combining a bold form with mahogany featuring a striking grain, this brick fireplace incorporates an unusual horseshoe arch (derived from Islamic architecture) into its opening. Although most of the detailing in this 1911 house is in Craftsman style, the pair of large, scrolled wooden brackets and the rounded corners of the mantel are other variations. The wall sconces are contemporary additions.

🐝 27. *(right)* An original 1908 feature of an all-redwood living room with a peaked roof is this prized fireplace. A rather plain background of irregular clinker brick was used as a foil for the graceful shape of a hand-hammered copper hood, designed with intentionally visible rivets by period metal artisan D'Arcy Gaw (an early partner of Dirk Van Erp). Seemingly suspended from the cantilevered mantel are two overlay straps chemically patinated to a dark finish.

❧ 28. *(left)* In an unusual ensemble of artistry and handicraft, this living room fireplace, circa 1911, is both restrained and bold. Depicting a pipe-playing figure, the subtle relief carved into the brickwork (by sculptor John Stanbough Souther) relies mostly on angled light to fully reveal its fanciful imagery. Between the pair of built-in cushioned benches, a robust hand-crafted copper-and-iron hood spans the fireplace.

❧ 29. This detail of a 1912 fireplace shows how its plain, buff-colored-brick face is enhanced by a handwrought iron hood. A built-in bench at right offers comfortable fireside seating. Curves in the hood and the arm of the bench offset the room's otherwise straight lines.

❦ 30. Once centered in a shallow inglenook (between a pair of facing benches that have since disappeared), this 1907 fireplace remains a superb example of Arts and Crafts design. The strong color of its full-height, matte-glazed ceramic tile facing is in harmony with the finely executed iron strapping and hand-hammered copperwork of both the small hood and the ovenlike doors above it (which hide the damper mechanism).

🐝 31. Contrasting textures and colors of brick enliven this bungalow fireplace facing, which is framed by distinctive Craftsman-style wood detailing that high-lights the upper corners. The original hearth was damaged and has been replaced with new glazed ceramic tile.

🐾 32. The dark, recessed brickwork in the design of this 1916 bungalow's fireplace incorporates an unusual original panel of lighter-colored brick above the mantel. The Chinese calligraphy (which translates "Where art and books meet") and the pair of wall sconces are additions that lend a more contemporary feeling to the room.

🐾 33. Inset above a broad fireplace mantel in a rather modest 1910 bungalow living room is this original handcrafted copper panel. Depicting a leafy landscape, it shows the repoussé technique, in which the design is worked into the metal from the back. Its deeply beveled wood frame is recessed into horizontal stained fir boards.

34. Lacking a mantel, this fireplace features a shallow recessed panel in its plain brick facing. The current owner had the brick ledge inscribed with the first line of the Doxology and thus continues an English Arts and Crafts tradition of incorporating calligraphy of a favorite literary or biblical quotation into a room's decorative scheme to personalize it.

🐝 35. A continuous mantel unifies neighboring built-ins and this fireplace, faced with matte-finished tile in a warm, neutral color in harmony with the William Morris-designed wallpaper. The diagonal lines of the accent tiles are echoed in the fireplace fender, the peaked open doorway, and the glass doors of the built-in bookcase. A small drop-front desk abuts the fireplace.

Wallpaper by Bradbury & Bradbury

🐝 36. Now separated from an adjoining living room only by a dropped beam, this room-wide inglenook is most likely missing its original colonnade (short columns set on low walls, used to divide a room or inglenook from an adjacent space). A mottled deep green and amber glaze on the ceramic tile of the fireplace facing blends well with the woodwork.

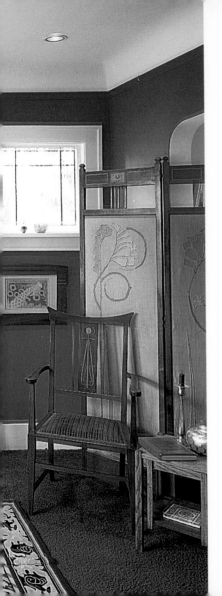

🐾 37. Rising to a gracefully coved ceiling, the chimney of this 1920s fireplace first curls inward around a small arched display niche. The similarly shaped fireplace opening has a matte-glazed tile surround, in the style of famed Arts and Crafts tile maker Ernest Batchelder, with pictorial tiles to accent the distinctive stepped arrangement.

🐘 38. A simple surround and hearth are faced with matte-glazed, mottled-finish ceramic tile. Above, a trio of charming low-relief pictorial tiles is inset across the front of the Craftsman-style mantel in this 1912 den. The tile images—old-fashioned tavern scenes with people in period costumes—suggest Colonial Revival influence. The small opening indicates that the fireplace was intended to burn coal.

🐾 39. Original and intact details on this strong but restrained 1913 Craftsman-style fireplace design make it exceptional. From the overhang of its top shelf, two handcrafted copper lanterns are artfully suspended. Above the cantilevered mantel, a single large pictorial landscape tile is inset to one side of the plain brick facing.

🐨 40. In the distinctive style of master tile maker Ernest Batchelder, authentic period tiles with low-relief pictorial decoration are combined with reproduced matte-glazed field tiles to create a new surround and hearth for this rebuilt bedroom fireplace. A straightforward Craftsman-style mantel allows the tiles to take center stage.

🐨 41. Below a mantel of matching glazed ceramic pieces, a low-relief, matte-glazed pictorial Claycraft tile accents the plain brick-and-tile face of a 1920s fireplace. Set in a small Spanish Baroque-style frame is a romantic scene of an early California mission.

❦ 42. Glazed ceramic tile fireplace components with an aged finish offering instant "character" were popular in the 1920s and sold through catalogs. Imitations of Ernest Batchelder's work, these tiles, including the corbel and the peacock accent tile, were actually made by Calco Tile.

❦ 43. Another view of the all-tile fireplace in Figure 42 shows its keystone and a large central accent panel depicting peacocks and squirrels intertwined in a stylized oak tree. A small metal-tasseled chain between the panel and the keystone operates the chimney's flue..

🐝 44. A bedroom fireplace in the 1909 Thorsen House in Berkeley, California, designed by Greene and Greene, artfully employs rounded and pegged Port Orford cedar elements, polished steel bars, and a Rookwood tile surround accented with tiny mosaics.

🐝 45. While its woodwork and tile designs are similar to those in Figure 44, this bedroom fireplace in Greene and Greene's 1908 Gamble House in Pasadena, California, has a shelf above the mantel between a pair of display cabinets with leaded glass doors.

🐝 46. Below a bracketed Craftsman-style mantel, handmade tiles face both front and sides of this 1912 fireplace. The mottled glaze, a combination of reddish brown and deep green, harmonizes well with the tones of the adjacent wood.

❦ 47. With its palette in shades of deep ochre and its diverse textures of dripping glaze, the tile facing of this Craftsman-style fireplace exudes a handmade quality typical of the Arts and Crafts aesthetic that is also seen in some art pottery of the period.

❦ 48. The particular shade of green on the large matte-glazed ceramic tiles facing this 1914 fireplace is often associated with the Grueby Pottery. Beneath a darkly stained mantel are the original brass corner guards and screen hardware.

🐝 49. With a flattened Tudor arch at its opening and stylized pinwheel forms accenting its green tile face, this 1907 fireplace shows British Arts and Crafts influences. The versatility of ceramic materials for architectural applications is apparent in the arch.

❦ 50. Through the iron grille of a small window in the front door, a softly lit setting in front of a cozy inglenook is revealed, exuding the timeless appeal of good friends and good cheer by a warm fireside.

Pillow by Carol Mead Design

BUNGALOW BACKGROUND

America's most popular house of the early twentieth century, the bungalow, is making a big comeback as our newest "historic" house. Surviving bungalows are now considered treasures by historic preservationists, while homeowners rediscover the bungalow's appeal as a modest, practical home with a convenient floor plan. This book highlights an important aspect of bungalow interiors.

Webster's New Collegiate Dictionary describes a bungalow as "a dwelling of a type first developed in India, usually one story, with low sweeping lines and a wide verandah." The word *bungalow* derives from the Hindi *bangala,* both an old Hindu kingdom in the Bengal region of India and a rural Bengali hut with a high thatched-roof over-hang creating a covered porch (or verandah) around the perimeter to provide shade from the scorching sun. The height and steep pitch of the roof encouraged the hottest air to rise and escape, while cooler air flowed in at ground level (especially after sundown). The British colonists adapted the design in their own dwellings, and their success spread the concept from India to elsewhere in the British Empire, especially Southeast Asia, Africa, New Zealand, and Australia. By the late eighteenth century, the name *bangala* had been anglicized to *bungalow.*

This name first appeared in print in the United States in 1880. Used in an architectural journal, it described a single-story, shingled Cape Cod summerhouse ringed by covered porches. By the 1900s, *bungalow* had become part of our popular vocabulary, at first associated with vacation homes, both seaside and mountain. The bungalow's informality, a refreshing contrast to stuffy Victorian houses, helped fuel its popularity as a year-round home. It had its greatest fame as a modest middle-class house from 1900 to 1930.

Widely promoted, the bungalow was touted for its modernity, practicality, affordability, convenience, and often-artistic design. Expanding industry and a favorable economy across the country created an urgent need for new, affordable, middle-class housing, which the bungalow was just in time to meet.

In America, a bungalow implied a basic plan, rather than a specific style, of modest house. Typically, it consisted of 1,200 to 1,500 square feet, with living room, dining room, kitchen, two bedrooms, and bathroom all on one level. Some bungalows had roomy attic quarters, but most attics were bare or intended to be developed as the family's needs grew. A bungalow set in a garden fulfilled many Americans' dream of a home of their own.

Widely publicized California bungalows in the early 1900s spawned frenzied construction in booming urban areas across the country. In design, most bungalows built prior to World War I adopted the so-called Craftsman style, sometimes combined with influences from the Orient, the Swiss chalet, or the Prairie style. After the war, public taste shifted toward historic housing styles, and bungalows adapted Colonial Revival, English cottage, Tudor, Mission, and Spanish Colonial Revival features.

Today Craftsman is the style most associated with bungalows. Characterized inside and out by use of simple horizontal lines, Craftsman style relies on the artistry of exposed wood joinery (often visible on front porch detailing). Natural or rustic materials (wood siding, shingles, stone, and clinker brick) are favored. Interiors may be enriched with beamed ceilings, high wainscot paneling, art glass, and hammered copper or metalwork lighting accents.

The word *Craftsman* was coined by prominent furniture manufacturer and tastemaker Gustav Stickley, who used it to label his line of sturdy, slat-backed furniture (also widely known as Mission style), which was influenced by the English Arts and Crafts movement. That movement developed in the mid-nineteenth century as a reaction against the Industrial Revolution. Early leaders such as John Ruskin and William Morris turned to the medieval past for inspiration as they sought to preserve craft skills disappearing in the wake of factory mechanization.

In both the decorative arts (furniture, wallpaper, textiles, glass, metalwork, and ceramics) and architecture, the Arts and Crafts movement advocated use of the finest natural materials to make practical and beautiful designs, executed with skillful handcraftsmanship. One goal was to improve the poor-quality, mass-produced home furnishings available to the rising middle class. Morris and a group of like-minded friends founded a business to produce well-designed, handcrafted goods for domestic interiors. Although the company aspired to make its goods affordable to all, it faced the inevitable conflict between quality and cost. However, its Arts and Crafts example inspired many others in England (and eventually in America) to relearn treasured old craft traditions and continue them for posterity.

As it grew, the movement also became involved in politics, pressing for social reforms. Factory workers trapped in dull, repetitive jobs (with little hope for anything better) were among their chief concerns; they saw the workers' fate as a waste of human potential and talent.

The idealistic and visionary English movement's artistic goals of design reform were more successful than its forays into social reform. Perhaps its greatest success, in both England and the United States, was in giving the public a renewed sense of the value of quality materials, fine craftsmanship, and good design in times of rapid world change.

The Arts and Crafts movement had multiple influences on the

American bungalow. The movement arrived here from England in the early 1900s, just as the bungalow was becoming popular. Among its most successful promoters was Elbert Hubbard, founder of the Roycroft Community, a group of artisans producing handmade books and decorative arts inspired by Morris. Hubbard also published two periodicals and sold goods by mail order.

Gustav Stickley was another American inspired by England's important reform movement and soon was expressing this inspiration in the sometimes austere but well-made designs of his Craftsman style. Becoming an influential promoter of the bungalow as an ideal "Craftsman home," he marketed furniture, lighting, metalwork, and textiles styled appropriately for it. His magazine, *The Craftsman,* was a popular vehicle for his ideas and products, and he sold plans for the Craftsman houses he published in his magazine. The wide popularity of his Craftsman style spread the aesthetic sensibilities of the Arts and Crafts movement into countless American middle-class households, making it a growing influence on architecture and decorative arts here. (England in the early twentieth century remarkably had no middle-class housing form comparable to the American bungalow, but Australia has bungalows of that period, inspired by ours, rather than any from Britain.)

Other manufacturers eventually contributed to Stickley's downfall by blatantly copying his ideas and products and eroding his market share. Once Stickley's exclusive brand name, the word *Craftsman* was assimilated into general use and became public property after his bankruptcy in 1916.

Americans choosing the Craftsman style for their homes, interiors, and furnishings rarely were committed to the artistic and philosophical reforms of the Arts and Crafts movement; most were simply following a vogue. Prospective homeowners (and real estate developers) usually selected their bungalow designs from inexpensive sets of plans marketed in catalogs called plan books; few used an architect's services. Some people even bought prefabricated "ready-cut" or "kit" houses. First sold in 1909 by Sears, Roebuck and Company, prefabricated houses soon were widely copied. In the heat of bungalow mania, Sears and others offered tempting incentives to prospective bungalow buyers, such as bonus financing for their lots. For a time, it was said that if you had a job, you could afford a bungalow. But when jobs were in short supply as the Great Depression hit, many defaulted on their little dream homes, leaving their creditors stung.

The depression ended the heyday of the bungalow, but its practical innovations reappeared in later houses, then more likely to be called cottages. The post-World War II ranch house could be considered the legacy of the bungalow. Only recently has a rising demand for lower-cost houses triggered a reevaluation of vintage bungalow stock as viable housing. In response to public demand, the home planning and construction industries have reprised some of the obvious charms of the bungalow in new homes. A real boon for homeowners seeking to restore or renovate a vintage bungalow (or perhaps build a new one) is today's flourishing Arts and Crafts revival, fueled by the demand for a wide array of newly crafted home furnishings that reflect the traditions and spirit of the Arts and Crafts movement.